WHOOPI'S BIG BOOK OF MANNERS

ISBN-13: 978-0-545-07732-3
ISBN-10: 0-545-07732-X

Text copyright © 2006 by Whoopi Goldberg.
Illustrations copyright © 2006 by Olo. All rights reserved.
Published by Scholastic Inc., 557 Broadway, New York, NY 10012, by arrangement with Hyperion Books for Children, an imprint of Disney Children's Book Group, LLC. SCHOLASTIC and associated logos are trademarks and/or registered trademarks of Scholastic Inc.

12 11 10 9 8 7 6 5 4 3 2 1   8 9 10 11 12 13/0

Printed in the U.S.A.   08

First Scholastic printing, February 2008

WHOOPI'S BIG BOOK OF MANNERS

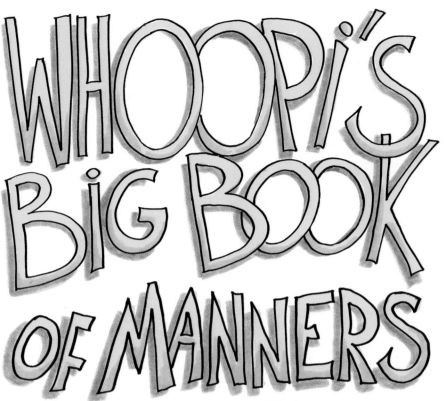

By WHOOPI GOLDBERG

Pictures by OLO

SCHOLASTIC INC.
New York Toronto London Auckland Sydney
Mexico City New Delhi Hong Kong Buenos Aires

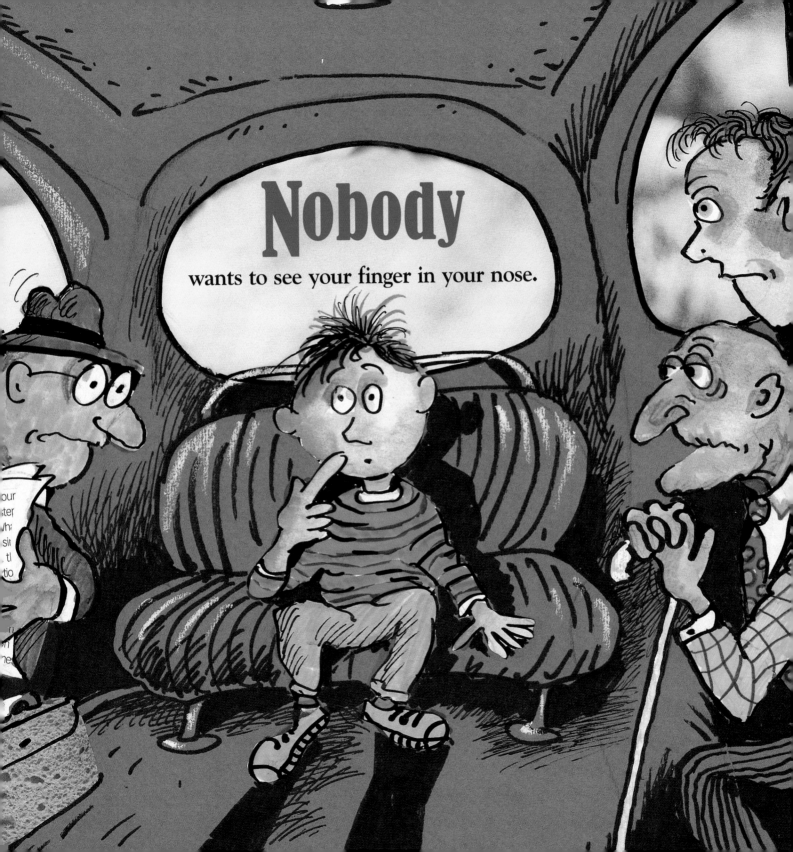

But before we get to that,

let's start with these special words.
They're special because they're polite
and too rarely heard. Don't forget to use them.

But forgetting to use these words is not as bad as . . .

Interrupting.

You're in the middle of a great story, and your kitty-cat decides to interrupt you with a loud "Meow." You say, "Oh, hello, nice kitty," and continue your story.

But again Kitty interrupts: "MEOW."
You say, "Nice kitty," and go on talking.
"ME-OOO-W!"
You look at Kitty, annoyed because you were in the middle of a great story, and realize Kitty is holding a suitcase and a shovel: you've forgotten to clean Kitty's litter box. You explain to Kitty that if she had just said "Excuse me," things would have happened a lot quicker.

But interrupting is not as bad as . . .

Forgetting to Clean Up After Yourself.

If you've just made a nine-layer double-fudge, marshmallow, strawberry, white-cream cake, and you used every pot in the kitchen and there is flour everywhere, do not touch the walls or go sit on the couch and watch TV. Clean up after yourself so you can enjoy the cake before you go to bed. Procrastinating does not help.

But
forgetting
to clean up
after yourself is
not as bad as . . .

Coughing or Sneezing Without Covering Your Mouth.

Just because you feel okay and you think everyone is healthy because they are taking their echinacea *(ek-ah-nay'-sha)* and they are bundled up on cold days to protect themselves and you figure they won't get sick, cover your mouth anyway.

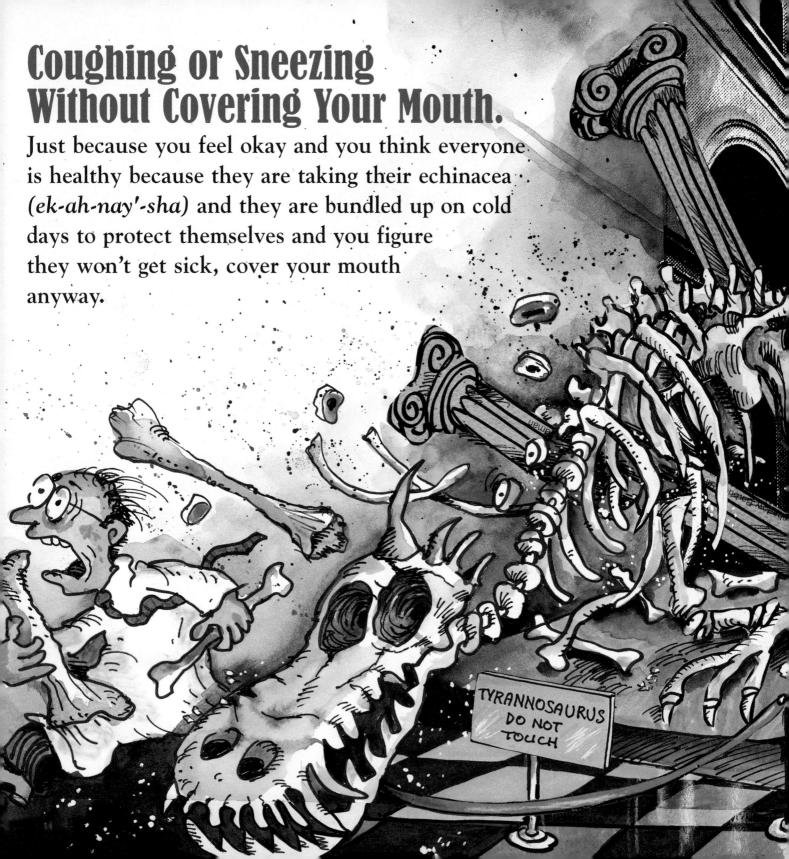

But coughing or sneezing without covering your mouth is not as bad as . . .

Forgetting to Knock on a Closed Door.

You never know if someone is doing an experiment or wrapping a birthday present. Or maybe they just want to be alone. Some surprises you just do not want to know about.

Knock on a closed door!

But forgetting to knock on a closed door is not as bad as . . .

Not Saying You're Sorry.

Don't pretend you don't know what's going on when you see everybody looking at you, tapping their feet, rolling their eyes, breathing hard and heavy. Be brave, ask the magic question: "Did I do something wrong?"

If you did, say "I'm sorry."

But not saying you're sorry is not as bad as . . .

Well, Lots of Things.

Especially at the table.

- Don't wipe your mouth with your hands. (If you don't have a napkin or tissue, use your shirtsleeve. Oh, wait, I take that back—excuse yourself from the table and get a napkin.)
- If you are eating creamed corn, oatmeal, peas, or mashed potatoes, do not use your hands (unless you are an ogre. In most cases, ogres are exempt from having certain table manners—it's a cultural thing . . .).
- Don't smack, chomp, or slurp at the table (unless you are from China—more on this later).
- Don't get into a burping contest (unless you are from Korea—more on that later too).
- Don't talk with food in your mouth.
- Don't lick your plate.

But not
having good
table manners is
not as bad as . . .

Bad Phone Manners.

If you are the caller, always say your name, ask to speak to the person you are calling, and end the sentence with "please."

Here's an example:

"Hello, this is Azalia Christmasbubble. May I speak to Odenda Finny, please?"

If the person you are calling is not at home or not available, say your name and number, clearly and slowly—especially if it's on an answering machine—so that she can call you back.

If you are the callee, and the call is not for you but for someone who is home and taking phone calls, say, "Would you please hold on?" Go and get the person; your job is done. If the person is not home, say, "Odenda is not at home. May I take a message?" WRITE IT DOWN. You know you're not going to remember it. Thank them for calling, put the message where the person can find it, and go about your day or evening.

But bad phone manners are not as bad as . . .

Bad Cellular Phone Manners.

Don't think Serena Williams would be happy at Wimbledon or Tiger Woods would not roar at the Masters if he heard your cell phone ring.

These are the worst places to be on your cellular phone:

- In a car.
- At a church or a mosque or a temple.
- In a library.
- At a sporting event.
- In a restaurant.

But having bad cellular phone manners is not as bad as . . .

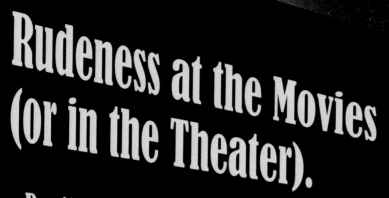

Rudeness at the Movies (or in the Theater).

- Don't talk—people can always hear you. (Whisper, if you must.)
- Unwrap your candy BEFORE the curtain goes up.
- Go to the bathroom BEFORE you take your seat.
- And turn off your PHONE!

But rudeness
at the movies
or in the theater
is not as bad as . . .

Being a Poor Sport.

THERE ARE SIX RULES FOR KIDS:
1. Be a considerate spectator.
2. Don't yell in other people's ears.
3. Cheer your team, but don't aggravate the people around you.
4. At all costs, avoid temper tantrums—they are not attractive.
5. Don't yell ugly words—it makes everybody feel bad.
6. Remember to congratulate the winner and compliment the loser, because we know everybody tries their best.

THERE IS ONE RULE FOR GROWN-UPS:

1. Don't yell at the coach because you think little Magilla is not getting enough playing time or you think you can do a better job. If you can do a better job, go get a team of your own to coach so that parents can yell at you because you are not putting little Pione in the game.

If you're a poor sport, your kid will be too. It's a vicious cycle (so somebody has to break it).

But being a poor sport is not as bad as . . .

Elevator Rudeness.

If you are in an elevator, even if you have never been in one before, and the buttons are calling you, DO NOT press all the buttons. Fight the urge—it could be one of the most difficult challenges of your life. DO NOT DO IT!

When the elevator doors open, give people enough time to get off the elevator before you try to get on. Never put perfume or cologne on before entering an elevator (or a plane).

And don't leave a stinky air biscuit behind you. Anywhere.

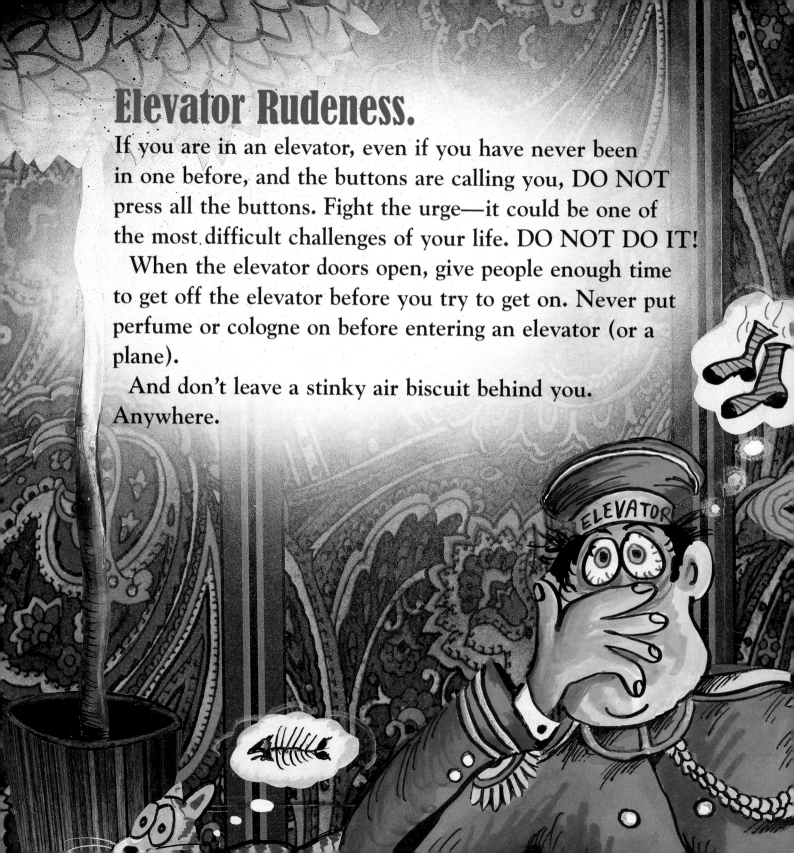

But elevator rudeness is not as bad as . . .

Doing Impolite Things When You Are in Another Country.

Here are some other good manners you should know about if you are traveling to other countries:

- In Asia, some people may bow instead of shaking hands. (Suggestion: Don't bow at the same time— you could knock each other out!)

- In Sweden, people never speak with raised voices. (Suggestion: Be prepared to stand really close and always carry breath freshener.)

- In Germany, it is impolite to put your hands in your lap during a meal. (As long as your hands aren't in your nose, they can go anywhere else.)

- In Korea, it is polite to belch at the table—it shows you enjoyed the meal. (Note: It's fine in Korea, but it may not go over well in other countries.)

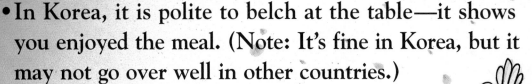

- In China, slurping your soup is common and not impolite. (Note again: It's fine in China, but it's not so fine most other places.)
- In Italy, friends will greet other friends with a kiss. (You might want to save some of that breath freshener from Sweden.)
- In Russia, if a woman whistles, it could be considered unladylike. (So would chewing tobacco.)
- In Japan, it is impolite to eat or drink something while walking down a street. (Except for cows, who are exempt.)

But even doing all those impolite things in all those foreign countries is not as bad as . . .

No. I can't say it.

Really, I better not. It's just too icky.

Okay, if you're going to make me . . .

Maybe, if you are alone,
in the privacy of your own home
or bathroom,
and not in a car, on a bus, or in a plane,
in school, on the roof, in the office,
watching TV, in the movies, or on an elevator,

it may be the only time . . .

you can stick your
finger up your nose.
But don't let anyone see!